m

TOWNSHIP OF RUSSELL PUBLIC LIBRARY
BIBLIOTHEQUE PUBLIQUE DU CANTON DE RUSSELL
SUCC. RUSSELL BRANCH

BIBLIOTHEQUE PUBLIQUE DU CANTON DE RUSSELL
TOWNSHIP OF RUSSELL PUBLIC LIBRARY
SUCC. MARIONVILLE BRANCH

BIG CATS

ANIMAL FAMILIES

BIG CATS

Markus Kappeler

Gareth Stevens Children's Books
MILWAUKEE

A N I M A L   F A M I L I E S

For a free color catalog describing Gareth Stevens' list of high-quality children's books, call 1-800-341-3569 (USA) or 1-800-461-9120 (Canada).

Picture Credits

Color illustrations are from Jacana (Switzerland) and Paris with the exception of the following: Bruce Coleman — Bartlett 24-25: Peter Davey 4-5, 29: Peter Jackson 19, 20: Plage 28, 30 (lower): Gunter Ziesler 26, 38, 39 (upper); EMB Service Archives — 7, 8, 9, 10 (upper), 10-11 (lower), 14; Federal Office of Veterinary Animals, Bern/Peter Dollinger — 15; Jurgen Klages — 34, 35; Okapia — Tom McHugh 32: Root 27; Zirkus Knie, Rapperswil — Chris Krenger 13: Rene Strickler 12.

Library of Congress Cataloging-in-Publication Data

Kappeler, Markus, 1953-
   [Grosskatzen. English]
   Big cats / Markus Kappeler.
      p. cm. — (Animal families)
   Translation of: Grosskatzen.
   "North American edition"—T.p. verso.
   Includes bibliographical references and index.
   Summary: Presents an evolutional and historical accounting of the cat family, as well as the physical attributes, life expectancies, native environments, and daily habits of its major members.
   ISBN 0-8368-0685-9
   1. Panthera—Juvenile literature. 2. Cheetahs—Juvenile literature. [1. Panthera. 2. Cats.] I. Title. II. Series: Animal families (Milwaukee, Wis.)
QL737.C23K3613   1991
599.74'428—dc20   91-9427

North American edition first published in 1991 by
Gareth Stevens Children's Books
1555 North RiverCenter Drive, Suite 201
Milwaukee, Wisconsin 53212, USA

This edition first published in 1991 by Gareth Stevens, Inc. Original edition copyright © 1988 by Kinderbuchverlag KBV Luzern AG, Lucerne, Switzerland, under the title *Grosskatzen*. Adapted by Gareth Stevens, Inc. All additional material supplied for this edition copyright © 1991 by Gareth Stevens, Inc. All rights to this edition reserved to Gareth Stevens, Inc. No part of this book may be reproduced, stored in a retrieval system, or transmitted in any form or by any means, electronic, mechanical, photocopying, recording, or otherwise, without the prior written permission of the publisher except for the inclusion of brief quotations in an acknowledged review.

Series editors: Amy Bauman and Patricia Lantier-Sampon
Editor: Russell Bennett
Designer: Sharone Burris
Translated from the German by: Jamie Daniel
Editorial assistants: Scott Enk, Diane Laska, and John Simons

Printed in the United States of America

1 2 3 4 5 6 7 8 9 95 94 93 92 91

Table of Contents

What Is a "Big Cat"?

Ancestors of today's cats were on the earth about forty million years ago. The cats that lived ten million years ago were very much like those that are alive today.

Cats belong to a large group of animals called carnivores. Carnivores are animals that eat meat. Scientists call this large group an order, and the name of this particular order is Carnivora. Some other carnivores are bears, wolves, pandas, and skunks.

Orders are divided into groups called families. Families may also have divisions, called subfamilies. Cats belong to the family whose scientific name is Felidae.

There are three major types of cats. Each type is called a genus. The genus discussed in this book contains the "big cats." The scientific name for this genus is *Panthera*.

In all, the family Felidae has about three dozen species, or kinds, of cats, many within the genus *Panthera*. Scientists don't agree on exactly how many species exist. Also, some scientists divide cats into three subfamilies, but others disagree on that, too.

The main reason that scientists have different opinions about cats is that cats are so much like each other. The lion with its mane, the lynx with its stubby tail, and the serval with its spotted coat are quite different in some ways, but anyone who looks at them knows that they are cats. In other animal families, members may not look alike. Who would guess, for instance, that otters, badgers, and weasels all belong to the same family? In that family, it is easy for scientists to decide how many species there are.

Above and opposite: The lion is a powerful creature with jaws that can break a buffalo's neck and a roar that can be heard for miles. This animal has been feared and honored for centuries. This is evident in the lion-demon shown above, which was carved over five thousand years ago in Persia.

Since cats are so similar, however, scientists must use small, seemingly unimportant details to distinguish one species from another. And because the details are small, it is easy to disagree about them.

This book will not deal with any of the disagreements. Rather, it will focus on one cat genus that is accepted by most scientists: the genus *Panthera* — the big cats: tigers,

Big cats have played a role in art, religion, and legends throughout the ages for many different peoples. Left: "Roaring Lion," by an Etruscan goldsmith, southern Italy, 700 B.C. Below: The "Dancing Jaguar Man," a Maya Indian wall drawing, comes from pre-Columbian Central America.

lions, leopards, jaguars, and snow leopards. It will also look at the cheetah, a cat that is very much like the big cats but isn't one.

Is It a Big Cat or a Small Cat?

Some of the characteristics that have been used to distinguish the big cats from others simply don't do the job. Size, for example, is not enough. Big cats certainly are large, but the puma is classified as a small cat, even though it is as large as the leopard. The shape of the pupil of the eye in bright light has also been suggested as a determining factor. Big cats usually have round pupils, and small cats usually have narrow, vertical slits. But there are exceptions here as well. The lynx has round pupils, and yet it belongs to the small cats. Feeding position is also a way to distinguish the two kinds of cats. Generally, big cats feed while lying down, and small cats stand up to eat. But once again, at least one big cat type doesn't fit the rule. The snow leopard feeds like a small cat.

There is only one characteristic that clearly differentiates big cats from other cats. That is a small, horseshoe-shaped bone at the base of the tongue. This bone, called the hyoid bone, connects the tongue to the skull. The hyoid bone of big cats has an elastic section, while that of other types of cats is completely hard.

Because of their elastic hyoid bone, big cats can purr only when they exhale. The flexible hyoid bone is what allows big cats to roar. The lion and the tiger are the masters of roaring. But anyone who has ever heard a leopard call out from the deep forest knows that even this big cat has a heart-stopping roar. Oddly enough, even though the snow

The "Winged Lion" comes from a woodcut created by the German painter and engraver Albrecht Dürer in 1498.

"Hercules Fighting with the Nemean Lion" is an example of detailed artwork from the Roman Empire, A.D. 600.

leopard has an elastic hyoid bone, it never roars. From this point on, this book will look at how big cats are alike and how they live.

Perfect Predators

Meat-eating animals are predators that hunt and eat other animals. The big cats have always been predators. Forty million years ago, the saber-toothed tiger sought prey in the primitive forest. In the millions of years that have passed since then, the big cats' skill in catching prey has nearly reached the level of perfection.

The big cats have superior eyesight. This feature contributes greatly to their skill as predators. For one thing, big cats can focus on very small details. Their eyes are extremely sensitive to light, which is why big cats can see so well at twilight and even at night. What allows cats to see so well is a layer of special tissue that is behind the eye's sensory cells. This special tissue is called the *tapetum lucidum*, which means "luminous carpet."

People see things when light rays enter the eye and are absorbed by the eye's sensory cells. These cells form a membrane known as the retina. However, not all light rays are absorbed by the retina. In a cat, some of the rays that are not absorbed hit the tapetum. Those rays bounce off the tapetum and go into the retina for a second time. In a way, this means that cats see everything twice. If you've ever stood in front of a cat in the dark or under other low-light conditions, you have probably noticed its glowing eyes. What you are actually seeing are the light rays that have bounced off the tapetum lucidum.

Another feature that makes the big cats good predators is their large, muscular paws. Big-cat paws are like traps made of muscle, tendons, and razor-sharp claws. With them, a cat grasps its prey and flings it to the ground. Once a cat has snared a victim, it almost never escapes. But the claws extend only when the cat is catching prey or climbing. While walking, the cat pulls its crescent-

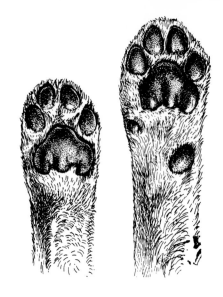

Right: Cats walk on their toes. On a cat's front paw (pictured right), there are five toes. The "thumb" is small and doesn't touch the ground. On the back paws (pictured left), cats have only four toes. The big toe has regressed.

Below: As this chart shows, cats come in all different sizes. Pictured from left to right: a lion, a Bengal tiger, a leopard, a clouded leopard, a lynx, an ocelot, and a house cat.

shaped claws back into pockets of skin. In this way, the claws always stay sharp.

The teeth of the big cats are also well suited to catching prey. The powerful, pointed canine teeth are about 1 inch (2.5 cm) longer than the other teeth. These daggerlike teeth allow the big cats to kill their prey with a single, powerful bite. Cats' molars are also sharp. Plant-eating animals have dull molars with which they chew food. The cats' sharp molars, however, are used to cut off bite-sized pieces of flesh from their victims as if with a scissors.

Maintaining Nature's Balance

Some people are repelled by the image of a big cat pouncing on a helpless animal and killing it. Actually, big cats kill only for food, and it has been shown that they never kill more animals than they are able to eat. When they are hungry, big cats strike prey and eat it over the next few days. In a real sense, predators like the big cats are no different from the frog that catches flies in the mud, the hedgehog that hunts for snails along the edge of the garden path, or the wren that looks for butterfly eggs on a moss-covered branch. They are all simply eating.

Whenever big cats kill prey, they are fulfilling an important task in nature. Some of their victims may be weak, sick, or fragile. Killing these animals checks the spread of disease and also prevents animals with weak characteristics from reproducing. Thus, the big cats contribute to the health of their prey as well as to their ability to survive.

Symbols of Power and Dignity

Since the beginning of history, big cats have had an almost magical effect on people. The reasons for this may lie in our fear of these

Right: In low light, a cat's pupils open into wide circles (upper photo). In bright light, the pupils of most small cats appear as slits. The pupils of most big cats, however (lower photo), simply become smaller circles.

dangerous animals as well as our admiration of their magnificence. For many centuries, big cats have had an important role in the legends, dances, and customs of numerous peoples the world over.

The lion, the "king of the beasts," has probably played this role more than any other big cat. Throughout the world, the lion has been and is a symbol of power and dignity. The Bible tells us that three thousand years ago, the throne of King Solomon was surrounded by fourteen carved lions. Today, the lion embellishes the coats of arms of many royal families, including those of England, Norway, and Denmark.

In many places, the leopard is another symbol of great dignity. For example, Mobuto Sese Seko, president of Zaire, wears a leopard-skin cap at official government functions. And King Jigme Singye Wangchuk of Bhutan receives his guests in a room that is decorated with leopard skins.

In many religions, big cats are symbols of great dignity. In Hinduism, for instance, the god Vishnu appears as half man and half lion. Bastet, the cat-goddess of the ancient Egyptians, has the head of a lioness, inspiring fear and promising protection at the same

The long whiskers of the big cats act as antennae and have something to do with a cat's sense of space. But even today, scientists do not fully understand all of what the whiskers do.

Township of Russell Public Library
Bibliothèque publique du canton de Russell

time. For the Inca, the jaguar was the embodiment of strength, courage, and agility. It was honored on the same level as Vovacocha, the Inca god of creation.

Becoming Endangered

With the invention of firearms, the big cats lost some of their power over humans. For the first time, people were more powerful than the predators. Shepherds could protect their flocks from the attacks of the big cats. And a wealthy person who wanted a lion-skin rug could easily get one. For a long time, the hunting of big cats by ranchers who wanted to protect their herds or by trophy hunters did not have too much of an effect on the population of the big cats. But when fur coats became fashionable, the demand for pelts increased dramatically. Professional hunters systematically sought the big cats to meet the demand. The big cats — as well as other animals — were pursued into even the most remote corners of their habitats.

Campaigns by international nature and environmental organizations brought attention to this situation in the late 1960s. Their efforts had tangible results in 1973 when the International Agreement on Trade in Endangered Animals and Plants went into effect. One result of that agreement was the outlawing of trade in big-cat pelts. Thanks to this agreement, which was endorsed by ninety-five countries, hunting is no longer a serious danger to these animals.

Today, however, many animals are threatened by other factors. For one thing, there has been an increase in the destruction of their natural habitats for human uses. At the same time, the severe decrease in the animals the big cats need for food contributes to the decrease of the number of big cats. Fortunately, many countries have created sanctuaries in which the big cats can live naturally and relatively undisturbed.

Previous spread: Big cats have shown that they can be trained. They are careful observers that respond to the slightest changes in vocal tone, body language, or facial expression. The big cats' combination of intelligence and strength has long fascinated people. These features make big cats a favorite among circus acts.

In this drawing of a tiger from Korea, the artist has given the cat slit pupils. As mentioned earlier, big cats have round pupils.

A Guide to *Big Cats*

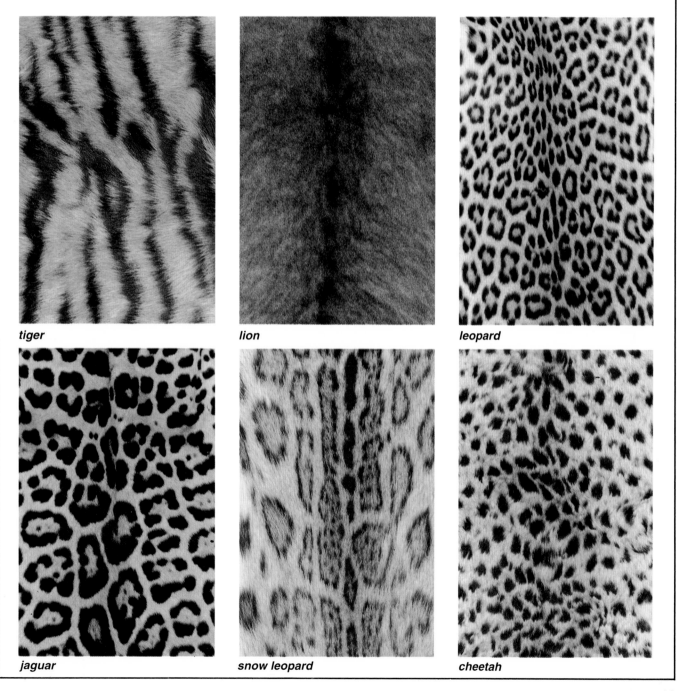

tiger

lion

leopard

jaguar

snow leopard

cheetah

The Tiger

Scientific name: Panthera tigris

Total length: 8-13 feet (2.4-3.9 m)
Tail length: 28-39 inches (71-100 cm)
Height at shoulder: 30-45 inches (75-115 cm)
Weight: 242-705 pounds (110-320 kg)
Gestation period: 95-113 days
Size of litter: 1-7 cubs; usually 2-4
Life expectancy: in the wild, 18-20 years;
*   in captivity, up to about 25 years*

The tiger lives primarily in southern Asia. In that expanse, which can be seen on the map at the back of this book, the tiger lives in a variety of habitats. It can be found in the sparse pine forests of the Russian taiga and in the bamboo thickets of China. It also lives in the flooded mango groves of the Ganges River delta in India and in the tropical jungles of Indochina. The tiger makes no particular demands on its environment. All it needs is enough prey to feed itself, a year-round supply of water for drinking, and enough cover to hide itself when stalking its prey.

There are eight subspecies of tigers. They are listed in the box on page 20. The subtypes can be distinguished from one another primarily by their body size, hair length, basic coloring, and the pattern of their stripes. Within each subtype, however, these physical characteristics vary considerably, so it is difficult, even for an expert, to classify a tiger without having additional information.

The Siberian tiger is the only one that is markedly different from the other subtypes. This tiger's winter coat is very long, and the animal is especially large and heavy. In fact, it is about one-fifth larger and heavier than the Bengal tiger. Indeed, the Siberian tiger is the largest of all the big cats. As with other tigers, as well as almost all other kinds of

Above: During the day, the tiger often finds a shady spot to rest.
Opposite: At night, the tiger goes in search of prey. It crosses its territory on padded soles and often covers great distances.

cats, the male tiger is bigger and heavier than the female.

A Solitary Hunter

The tiger usually lives and hunts alone. If there is a sufficient food supply, the tiger stays in one area, often for its whole life. The size of the tiger's territory depends on how much food is available. For example, in areas in India that have many prey animals, the tiger's territory ranges from about 75 square miles (194 sq km) to 130 square miles (337 sq km). In Siberia, which has a much smaller animal population, the tiger's area may be over 1,380 square miles (3,585 sq km). The

territories of neighboring tigers may overlap somewhat, but the tigers will try to avoid each other. Tigers can tell when they are in a neighbor's area by the scent of urine which the neighbor has left. If a tiger comes across the fresh scent of a neighbor, it will usually leave the area.

From time to time, male and female tigers come together in order to mate. To find each other at that time, they give long roars that can be heard for miles through a nighttime silence. A pair of tigers parts soon after mating. The male tiger does not take part in raising the young.

After a gestation period of about one hundred days, the tigress usually gives birth to two to four cubs. At birth, the little tigers weigh about 2 pounds (1 kg), and, as with all young cats, their eyes are shut. In about a week, the cubs' eyes open. When the cubs are about eight months old, they go with their mother when she hunts for prey. The cubs stay with her until they reach about twenty months of age. After that, they head out on their own.

The tiger hunts at night, silently patrolling its territory. In one night, a tiger may cover more than 20 miles (32 km). The tiger swims across brooks and rivers effortlessly and without hesitation. The tiger hunts deer, antelope, wild pigs, and other medium-sized hoofed animals. When the tiger finds prey, it will creep up to the animal until it is about 40 feet (12 m) away. Then the tiger suddenly unleashes its strength and springs forward with two or three powerful strides.

With its great paws, the tiger grasps the prey and throws it to the ground. Then, with one powerful bite, the big cat either breaks the other animal's neck or strangles it to death. Not all of the tiger's attempts to catch prey are successful. Many would-be victims hear the big predator coming in time to run away. If the tiger does not catch its usual

prey during the night, it may turn on any animal, including porcupines, small rodents, birds, turtles, frogs, or even crabs. If a tiger is extremely hungry, it may go after more difficult prey, such as adult wild oxen, bears, or even elephants.

From studying tigers in zoos, zoologists know that they eat about 13 to 18 pounds (6-

Above: This is an example of the rare Sumatran tiger. The average Sumatran tiger is smaller than the Bengal tiger. It also has narrower stripes and a darker basic color.
Opposite: Tigers love the water. They frequently drink water, bathe in it on hot days, and effortlessly cross rivers and lakes.

8 kg) of meat a day. In the wild, this amount would be equal to about seventy deer-sized animals a year.

In general, tigers stay away from people. Occasionally, however, tigers do attack humans. In most cases, those tigers are old, sick, or injured, and people make easy prey. Healthy tigers usually attack humans only if they can no longer find enough prey within their territories. These cases are rare and are often blown out of proportion, so that in some places the tiger has become known as a dangerous killer of people.

An Endangered Animal

Today, the tiger is an endangered species. The destruction of its natural habitats, the reduction of its prey, and the hunting of

Above: "White tigers" are an extremely rare variation of the Indian tiger.
Opposite: With their long fur, these Siberian tigers are well adapted to their homes in cold climates. During mating season, males often compete for mates. As shown here, the competition often erupts into rough brawls.

tigers by humans are factors that have contributed to its decline.

Early in the twentieth century, more than 100,000 tigers existed throughout the world. By the early 1990s, the entire tiger population was estimated at no more than 8,000 animals. Three of the eight subspecies — the Balinese, Javanese, and Caspian tigers — have already disappeared from the earth. There is little hope for the Chinese tiger, of which there may be only 30 or 40 left. The chances for the

Siberian tiger are not too much better. About 300 or 400 of these animals are still known to exist. Sumatran tigers still number between 600 and 800 animals, so their future is somewhat brighter. There may also be as many as 2,000 Indochinese tigers.

Of all tigers, the Bengal tiger probably has the best chance for survival. Over the fifteen years between the late 1970s and the early 1990s, its numbers have grown from about 1,800 to about 5,000. Project Tiger is responsible for this encouraging situation. Project Tiger is a plan to save the tigers. The project was launched in 1972 by India's then prime minister, Indira Gandhi, and the World Wide Fund for Nature (formerly known as the World Wildlife Fund), a group whose purpose is to protect nature and natural resources. Among other things, Project Tiger set up fifteen sanctuaries for tigers in India. On these sanctuaries, which have a total area of about 9,500 square miles (24,700 sq km), tigers live undisturbed.

There are tigers in most zoos, and they reproduce on a regular basis. In the early 1990s, zoos throughout the world held 1,000 Siberian tigers, 60 pure-blooded Bengal tigers, and a few Sumatran and Chinese tigers.

Tiger Subgroups	
1. Caspian tiger	*Panthera tigris virgata* (extinct 1973)
2. Siberian tiger	*Panthera tigris altaica*
3. Chinese tiger	*Panthera tigris amoyensis*
4. Indochinese tiger	*Panthera tigris corbetti*
5. Bengal (Royal) tiger	*Panthera tigris tigris*
6. Sumatran tiger	*Panthera tigris sumatrae*
7. Javanese tiger	*Panthera tigris sondaica* (extinct 1978)
8. Balinese tiger	*Panthera tigris balica* (extinct 1937)

The Lion

Scientific name: Panthera leo

Total length: 7-11 feet (2.1-3.3 m)
Tail length: 28-41 inches (70-105 cm)
Height at shoulder: 30-45 inches (75-115 cm)
Weight: 265-550 pounds (120-250 kg)
Gestation period: 100-116 days
Size of litter: 1-6 cubs; usually 2 or 3
Life expectancy: in the wild, 16-20 years; in
   captivity, up to 25 years

Probably no animal has made a greater impression on human beings than the lion. The majesty, beauty, and strength of the "king of beasts" has impressed people throughout history. In the Middle East, for example, the lion was once looked upon as a god. And the lion has always been a symbol of animal power against which humans pit their strength. This was true three thousand years ago, when Egyptian pharaohs hunted lions for sport, in Roman times, when gladiators fought lions, and in modern times, when people have gone on safaris to hunt lions to prove their bravery.

A Pride of Lions

The fact that lions live in groups makes them different from the other big cats. Their groups are called prides. Prides usually consist of about two or three males and five to ten females, called lionesses, plus their cubs. Typical prides include roughly ten to twenty-five animals but may have as many as forty.

The adult lionesses form the core of the pride and are usually related to one another. They live together in the pride from the time they are born and usually stay in it until they die. The entire pride stays in a fixed territory that may remain unchanged for generations. The size of this territory depends on how many animals are available for prey. The

Above: Lion cubs come into the world with spotted coats. This coloring helps hide them in the brush of their habitat when their mothers must leave them to hunt.
Opposite: Lions like to settle near water, but they generally don't like to go in it. Here, a male and female lion easily jump a small stream. But will the cub land without getting wet?

areas may measure anywhere from 8 to 155 square miles (20-400 sq km). Unfamiliar females that enter the pride's territory are chased away by the pride's females. In some cases, the intruders may even be killed.

Generally, the male lions in the pride are not related to the females. In a sense, the

males are only guests in the pride. They do not take part in hunting for food, and they do not help care for the young. The males do participate in some activities, however. Their main job is to defend the pride against the attacks of roaming male lions. Sooner or later — usually every two or three years — a band of younger lions will succeed in chasing the resident males away. Then, in another few years, the newcomers themselves will suffer the same fate. Thus the male lions who live in the pride are continually being replaced. In the end, this changing is beneficial to all lions, since only the strongest males mate. That keeps the animals strong, a factor that is important for the survival of the species.

Mating Habits of the Lion

Lions, which can mate during any season, are ready to mate when they are four years old. The gestation period is about three and a half months. Shortly before it is time to give birth, the pregnant lioness leaves the pride. She goes to a private place that is protected from the sun and wind for her young to be born. Usually two or three cubs are born. For the first few weeks, the spotted baby lions move about awkwardly. By the time they are six to eight weeks old, they can walk. Their mothers then lead them into the pride, where other lionesses help care for them. Each mother takes special care of her own cubs, of course, but she will also nurse other cubs. Sometimes a hungry cub will wander from one lioness to another, drinking milk. The cub may visit three or four females before its hunger is satisfied. Sometimes lionesses who have no cubs wash and guard the youngsters. Even the males will reluctantly allow the young lions to play with them.

At the age of three months, the cubs first go with the pride on a hunt. Gradually they learn the difficult task of catching prey. Lions are not full-fledged hunters until they are two years old, and they are not full-grown until they are six.

As a rule, the young females remain in the pride into which they are born. The young males, however, always leave the pride. When they are about 3-1/2 years old and their manes begin to grow, they are chased away by the older males in the pride. The young lions then form groups of their own, perhaps with other outcasts. At the age of five or six, male lions begin to attack the males of other prides. If they are successful, they become part of that pride. By studying fights between male lions, experts have learned that the male's mane is more than decoration. The manes give protection against a rival's claws.

How Lions Eat

Any kind of grassland can serve as the lion's habitat. Lions may live as high as 13,000 feet (4,000 m) into the mountains, but they consistently avoid dense forests. The most important factor in choosing a territory is the availability of sufficient prey. Lions usually eat various types of antelope and gazelles as well as zebras and water buffalo. Water buffalo, however, can be three or four times heavier than a lion. Many inexperienced young lions lose their lives trying to bring down a water buffalo.

Lions are excellent hunters. They patiently stalk their prey, trying to stay under cover. When a lion gets fairly close to its prey, it storms down on the surprised animal and throws it to the ground. Lions may reach a speed of 37 miles (60 km) an hour during these lightning-quick attacks. Another method of hunting involves the whole group. Part of the pride hides in tall grass, while others form a wide curve around the prey. The lions in the curve attack the prey and

Gnus and zebras are among the main prey of lions. During the hunt, the cunning hunters spread out and drive the prey together.

drive it into the group hiding in the grass. Lions sometimes lie in wait for victims at watering holes. Lions may also steal prey from hyenas, leopards, or other predators.

Once the prey has been killed, the male lions come out to join the feast. Although the lions in the pride are usually friendly toward one another, they can become ruthless while feeding. They growl, snarl, and swipe at one another with their paws. Once all have filled their stomachs, peace returns to the pride.

Where Lions Live and Die

At one time, lions roamed throughout Africa. They were also found in eastern Europe and in most of southern Asia, from Turkey to

Above: If the hunt is a success, lions fill themselves. An adult male lion can eat up to about 65 pounds (30 kg) of meat in one sitting. After eating, the lions collapse in a heap to sleep it off.
Right: Life in the pride is usually quite peaceful. But under certain conditions, lions may become ruthless with one another.

Lion Subgroups	
1. Asian lion	*Panthera leo persica* (extinct 1930)
2. Indian lion	*Panthera leo goojratensis*
3. North African Berber lion	*Panthera leo leo* (extinct 1920)
4. Senegalese lion	*Panthera leo senegalensis*
5. Cameroon lion	*Panthera leo kamptzi*
6. Congolese lion	*Panthera leo azandica*
7. Ugandan lion	*Panthera leo nyanzae*
8. Lake Victoria lion	*Panthera leo hollisteri*
9. Masai lion	*Panthera leo massaica*
10. Angolan lion	*Panthera leo bleyenbergi*
11. Kalahari lion	*Panthera leo vernayi*
12. Transvaal lion	*Panthera leo krugeri*
13. Cape lion	*Panthera leo melanochaita* (extinct 1865)

India. By about A.D. 100, lions disappeared from Europe. Today, most lions live in Africa, south of the Sahara Desert.

At the turn of the twentieth century, Asian lions were nearly extinct. A few were saved, however, and today, about two hundred live in the Gir Wildlife Sanctuary in India. They are the only lions living in the wild outside of Africa. As the Asian lion disappeared, lions living in northern and far southern Africa also declined. Even so, in Africa today, the lion is not considered threatened. However, as long as the lion's home — the African savanna — continues to be used for agricultural and grazing purposes, the lion's future will remain in question.

The Leopard

Scientific name: Panthera pardus

Total length: 5.6-9.5 feet (1.7-2.9 m)
Tail length: 24-39 inches (60-100 cm)
Height at shoulder: 22-33 inches (55-85 cm)
Weight: 66-187 pounds (30-85 kg)
Gestation period: 90-105 days
Size of litter: 1-6 cubs; usually 2-3
Life expectancy: in the wild, 15 years;
   in captivity, up to 23 years

Of all the big cats, the leopard inhabits by far the largest area. It is found throughout Africa as well as in all of southern Asia and on the islands of Sri Lanka and Java.

Like the tiger, the leopard makes no special demands on its environment. This big cat is adaptable to a variety of habitats and makes its home wherever it finds enough prey animals to survive and sufficient cover to hunt them. Leopards are known to live in stony, near-desert regions, in dense rain forests, in humid river deltas, and in misty mountain forests.

The patterns of the spots of the leopard's coat vary a great deal. The spots on its back are normally arranged in a flowery pattern known as a rosette. But some leopards have large, ring-shaped spots with dots in the center, like those of jaguars. Other leopards are covered with many single spots, like those of cheetahs. The basic color of the coat also varies. The color ranges from a whitish base to the black of the well-known black panther. The length of the fur of leopards' coats also varies.

Because of the many differences in coloring, pattern, and fur length, thirty-one

The leopard is a quick and agile climber. With this skill, this big cat often successfully hunts for monkeys in the treetops.

subspecies of leopards have been named. (See the box on page 30.) Most scientists feel, however, that not even thirty-one divisions are enough to distinguish one leopard subgroup from another.

For a long time, experts thought that the so-called black panther made up a separate species of big cat. This is not the case. A close

The leopard is incredibly strong. It often drags prey that is heavier than itself up into the trees. The leopard does this so it won't have to share its catch with hyenas, vultures, or any of the other carrion-eaters.

look at some black panthers reveals that they too have typical leopard spots. In addition, zoos have reported that black and spotted cubs can appear in the same litter.

A Fierce Hunter
The leopard is usually a loner. It spends most of the day resting in the fork of a tree or in some other shaded spot and becomes active in the evening hours. Then, as soon as it is dark, the leopard sets off in search of prey.

The leopard is an excellent stalker and appears to be able to kill almost anything that crosses its path. This big cat's favorite prey includes warthogs, wild pigs, antelope, deer, and wild goats. But the leopard also eats rabbits, monkeys, jackals, rodents, birds, snakes, fish, and even insects. In fact, small animals make up the major portion of the leopard's diet. The number of larger prey animals that it devours in a year seldom amounts to more than twenty. And while leopards occasionally prey on people, as is the

Black leopards are popularly known as "black panthers." Many people believe that they are particularly wild animals. But black leopards behave the same way as leopards with spotted coats do.

case with tigers, the attacker is usually an old or injured animal.

Male and female leopards live separately throughout most of the year. The size of their territories ranges from about 10 to 465 square miles (25-1,200 sq km). Males and females come together only to mate. During these few days, they are very gentle with each other and even hunt together. Between 90 and 105 days after mating, the female leopard gives birth, usually to two or three cubs. For about 1.5 years, the female lovingly cares for her young. After that, they must take care of themselves. The cubs will not be full-grown until they are three or four years of age.

Leopard Subgroups

1. North African leopard	*Panthera pardus panthera*	17. Sinai leopard	*Panthera pardus jarvisi*
2. West African leopard	*Panthera pardus leopardus*	18. South Arabian leopard	*Panthera pardus nimr*
3. Congolese leopard	*Panthera pardus ituriensis*	19. Lower Asian leopard	*Panthera pardus tulliana*
4. Ruwenzori leopard	*Panthera pardus ruwenzori*	20. Caucasian leopard	*Panthera pardus ciscaucasia*
5. Cameroon leopard	*Panthera pardus reichenowi*	21. North Persian leopard	*Panthera pardus saxicolor*
6. Ethiopian leopard	*Panthera pardus adusta*	22. Middle Persian leopard	*Panthera pardus dathei*
7. Eritrean leopard	*Panthera pardus antinori*	23. Baluchistan leopard	*Panthera pardus sindica*
8. South Somalian leopard	*Panthera pardus nanopardus*	24. Indian leopard	*Panthera pardus fusca*
9. North Somalian leopard	*Panthera pardus brockmani*	25. Ceylonese leopard	*Panthera pardus otiya*
10. Egyptian leopard	*Panthera pardus pardus*	26. Nepalese leopard	*Panthera pardus pernigra*
11. Ugandan leopard	*Panthera pardus chui*	27. Kashmir leopard	*Panthera pardus millardi*
12. East African leopard	*Panthera pardus suahelica*	28. Outer Indian leopard	*Panthera pardus delacouri*
13. Zanzibar leopard	*Panthera pardus adersi*	29. Chinese leopard	*Panthera pardus japonensis*
14. South African leopard	*Panthera pardus shortridgei*	30. Amur leopard	*Panthera pardus orientalis*
15. Namibian leopard	*Panthera pardus puella*	31. Javanese leopard	*Panthera pardus melas*
16. Cape leopard	*Panthera pardus melanotica*		

The Leopard in Today's World

The leopard population has been greatly reduced during the twentieth century. The main cause of this was the hunting of the animals for their pelts. For example, over twenty thousand leopard pelts were taken from Africa in 1973 alone. Fortunately, severe restrictions were imposed upon the fur trade, and there are signs that the number of leopards has begun to increase.

Young leopards curl up into a ball whenever they are being carried by their mother.

30

The Jaguar

Scientific name: Panthera onca

Total length: 5-9 feet (1.6-2.8 m)
Tail length: 18-31 inches (45-80 cm)
Height at shoulder: about 28 inches (70 cm)
Weight: 77-364 pounds (35-165 kg)
Gestation period: 93-110 days
Size of litter: 1-4 cubs; usually 2
Life expectancy: in the wild, 15 years;
   in captivity, up to 22 years

The jaguar is the only big cat native to the Americas. Its territory ranges from Mexico in the north to Paraguay in the south. Within this area the jaguar usually lives in the wild, undisturbed forests and in the bush-covered savannas, which are less than 3,300 feet (1,000 m) above sea level.

At first glance, the jaguar doesn't seem much different from the leopard, for which it is often mistaken. But a closer look shows a number of differences. The jaguar is much stronger and more stockily built than the leopard. In addition, it has a shorter tail and shorter legs. Finally, the jaguar's coat is different from the leopard's. Usually, the spots on the jaguar's back are formed by a large dark ring within which there is a solid black spot.

The jaguar is typically a loner. The males and females live in separate territories. Jaguars know their territories very well and know where they will be most likely to find prey. The jaguar's territory can cover from about 6 square miles (15 sq km) to slightly more than 300 square miles (800 sq km). Their territories overlap quite a bit. Generally speaking, all the jaguars in a particular area avoid contact with others in the area.

From time to time, though, males and females come together to mate. Then the forests and savannas are filled with the growls

The Indians who live in the forests along the banks of the Orinoco River believe that the jaguar is an almost human creature because it is as clever a hunter as they are.

of the jaguars. After a gestation period lasting between 93 and 110 days, the female jaguar usually gives birth to a set of twins in a sheltered thicket. For about two years, the cubs stay with their mother, learning to stalk prey. When the young jaguars are three years old, they leave their mother and set out to find a territory of their own.

Where the Jaguar Lives

The jaguar prefers to live close to rivers, lakes, and swamps, since prey is usually more abundant in these areas. The jaguar goes out to hunt only after twilight, stalking medium-sized hoofed animals, such as tapirs, peccaries, and mazamas. But these animals are often scarce, and they are difficult to kill. So the jaguar usually has to settle for smaller

animals, such as pacas, capybaras and other large rodents, anteaters, armadillos, iguanas, and birds. Since the jaguar is an excellent swimmer, it can also successfully hunt in forest streams for crocodiles, river turtles, and even fish. The jaguar is also a good climber and likes to search tree branches for opossums, sloths, and howling monkeys.

Old Indian stories say that the jaguar sometimes catches fish by lying on a tree branch and moving its tail in and out of the water. When curious fish draw near, the jaguar is said to snatch them from the water with its front paws. These stories have never been confirmed, however.

At one time, there were fair numbers of jaguars in the southern United States, but they have died out over the past 130 years. The cat's reputation as a livestock killer has led to its decline. The last jaguar in California was shot in 1860, in Texas in 1946, and in

Jaguar Subgroups	
1. Amazonian jaguar	*Panthera onca onca*
2. Paraná jaguar	*Panthera onca palustris*
3. Peruvian jaguar	*Panthera onca peruviana*
4. Panamanian jaguar	*Panthera onca centralis*
5. Yucatán jaguar	*Panthera onca goldmani*
6. West Mexican jaguar	*Panthera onca hernandesi*
7. East Mexican jaguar	*Panthera onca veracrucensis*
8. Arizona jaguar	*Panthera onca arizonensis* (extinct 1949)

Arizona in 1949. During the 1960s, jaguars in Central America and South America were hunted for their pelts. In the Amazon Basin alone, about fifteen thousand jaguars were killed during that time. This slaughter has now been brought under control. But today the jaguar faces another danger as the tropical forests of Central and South America — the jaguar's habitat — continue to be destroyed.

Opposite: As is true of leopards, jaguars are sometimes born with all-black coats.
Below: Jaguar cubs can play for hours.

33

The Snow Leopard

With its teeth flashing and its ears flattened, this snow leopard makes an intimidating impression on intruders.

Scientific name: Panthera uncia

Total length: 6-8 feet (1.8-2.3 m)
Tail length: 33-43 inches (85-110 cm)
Height at shoulder: about 24 inches (60 cm)
Weight: 77-143 pounds (35-65 kg)
Gestation period: 96-105 days
Size of litter: 1-5 cubs; usually 2 or 3
Life expectancy: about 15 years

The snow leopard, also called the ounce, is a mountain cat. It lives in the Himalayas and other mountain ranges in central Asia. It is usually found above the treeline at altitudes from about 10,000 feet (3,000 m) to just over 13,000 feet (4,000 m). It sometimes goes as high as about 20,000 feet (6,000 m).

The snow leopard is smaller than the true leopard. It can be distinguished by its bright, extremely long, and thick coat, which has large, smoky gray ring-shaped spots. It also has a very long tail and huge paws. These three features are adaptations to the rocky slopes, crevices, and snow-covered surfaces of the environment that the snow leopard inhabits. The snow leopard's thick coat protects it from bitter cold and at the same time provides good camouflage. Its long tail serves as a sort of balancing pole as it wanders along narrow, rocky ridges. The tail also "steers" the animal when it jumps across crevices. And with its broad paws, it is able to find secure footing on even the steepest rocky cliffs. Its paws also act like snowshoes and prevent the snow leopard from sinking into deep snow.

Until the mid-1980s, next to nothing was known about the life of the snow leopard. That's not surprising. Its home is remote, and the animal is shy. Also, because of its unusual camouflage markings, even people who live in the snow leopard's habitat rarely see it. But between 1982 and 1985, a study done by researcher Rodney Jackson finally provided some information on the life of this mysterious big cat.

Scientists now know that the snow leopard lives alone. It normally hunts at night near villages. In areas where there is not enough prey, it may also hunt during the day. In hunting, the snow leopard hides among the big boulders of its habitat, waiting for prey. The big cat can easily leap up to these observation points because it is an incredible jumper. It can leap distances of up to 49 feet (15 m).

In the past, the snow leopard was thought to be a tireless wanderer who continuously crossed the boundless mountain areas of central Asia. This is not the case. Snow leopards occupy fixed territories, just as other big cats do. In Nepal's Langu Valley, for example, these territories range in area from about 8 to 12 square miles (20-30 sq km).

Snow leopards avoid contact with other snow leopards. The scent marks and scratch marks that they leave at conspicuous points along their paths tell others to stay away. But toward the end of winter, males and females come together to mate. Then, after a gestation period of 96 to 105 days, the female gives birth to two or three cubs in her hidden den. The cubs stay in the safe den for six to eight weeks. After that, they accompany their mother when she hunts. When the cubs are a year old, they strike out on their own.

Hoofed animals of all kinds make up the majority of the snow leopard's preys. But this cat can bring down just about anything that crosses its path, including animals that are three times its weight. Among its preys are sheep, mountain goats, thars, takins, gorals, and argali. Snow leopards also eat jack rabbits, marmots, and pheasants, white grouse, and other birds.

At one time, the snow leopard roamed over an area totaling about 385,000 square miles (1 million sq km). Today, it has become rare everywhere, and in many places, it has disappeared. It has been estimated that because of excessive killing by fur trappers and herders protecting their livestock, only about one thousand of these cats are left in the wild.

The snow leopard is quite at home in snowy, mountainous terrain. Its thick fur keeps it warm, even through the winter.

Not a Big Cat, Not a Small Cat

The Cheetah

Scientific name: Acinonyx jubatus

Total length: 6-8 feet (1.9-2.4 m)
Tail length: 26-33 inches (65-85 cm)
Height at shoulder: 28-33 inches (70-85 cm)
Weight: 88-165 pounds (40-75 kg)
Gestation period: 86-95 days
Size of litter: 1-6 cubs; usually 2-4
Life expectancy: about 15 years in the wild;
  up to 19 in captivity

The cheetah is not a big cat, so it really does not belong in this book. At the same time, the cheetah does not have the characteristics of the small cats. For these reasons, scientists consider the cheetah a separate species. In fact, the cheetah has a unique classification among cats. It is a part of the Felidae family, but it is the only member of its own subfamily, genus, and species. In a way, then, the cheetah is a bridge between big cats and small cats.

The cheetah hunts prey differently from all other types of cats. Instead of stalking and pouncing on its prey, the cheetah catches its prey by chasing it down in an open area. This is one reason that scientists consider the cheetah to be a separate species. Most of the physical characteristics that differentiate the cheetah from other cats have to do with its style of hunting.

The cheetah is famous for its ability to run at very high speeds. In three seconds, it can accelerate to a speed of 55 miles (89 km) per hour and can reach a top speed of about 70 miles (113 km) per hour. The cheetah's entire body is built for running. Its long, sinewy legs, its narrow paws with padded calluses, and its slender, streamlined body all contribute to its agility and speed. The cheetah

is the undisputed running champion of the animal kingdom.

It is interesting that the cheetah is the only cat that cannot retract its claws. Its claws remain extended and rub the ground each time the cat takes a step. Because of this, the cheetah's claws are constantly being worn dull, making the cheetah the only cat that cannot climb well. Although this feature may seem like a disadvantage, it also has its advantages. The cheetah's claws give the cat

Opposite: These young cheetahs will leave their mother only when they are between fifteen and seventeen months old. They have a lot to learn before they leave.
Below: The cheetah's build is very different from that of other cats in many ways. Among other things, it has a shorter jaw and smaller teeth.

excellent traction when it runs. The claws do for the cheetah what spiked shoes do for baseball or football players.

The cheetah usually hunts during the day. Again, this sets it apart from other cats. Its most frequent preys are small gazelles and antelope and occasionally an animal as large as a gnu or zebra. Once the cheetah has spotted its prey, it advances slowly, taking advantage of any cover. If the prey looks up, the cheetah stops and only advances again when the prey looks away. Finally, when the cheetah is about 165 feet (50 m) from the prey, it attacks with lightning speed. Like an arrow shot from a bow, the cheetah flies toward its goal. By the time the prey has sensed danger and bolted, the cheetah has covered half the distance between them. Seconds later, the prey is caught. With one powerful blow of its front paw, the cheetah throws the victim to the ground, biting its throat to kill it.

This fast runner doesn't always catch its prey, however. The cheetah can only maintain its speed for about 1,000 to 1,300 feet (300-400 m). If the prey has not been caught within this distance, the cheetah usually gives up. Even when the cheetah does catch its prey, it is often stolen by stronger rivals such as lions, leopards, hyenas, or wild dogs. These predators challenge the cheetah and will kill it if they have the opportunity. The cheetah is not only a predator, then; it is often itself the prey.

Above and opposite: A cheetah breaks into a run. Cheetahs can go from 0 to 55 miles (0-89 km) per hour in just three seconds.

A Very Different Kind of Cat

The cheetah's social life also differs from that of other cats. The adult females live alone and are usually accompanied only by their cubs. The males, on the other hand, often band together with their brothers and form packs of two to four animals.

The female and male groups live in fixed, overlapping territories. They range in area from 19 to 60 square miles (50-155 sq km). Groups avoid contact with their neighbors. Scent marks of urine tell one group that another is near.

The males and females meet only to mate. After a gestation period of about ninety days, the female gives birth to as many as six cubs. The cubs are born with silvery gray manes that they will have until they are about ten weeks old. Their manes camouflage them in the high grass, in which they hide during their first three months of life. Nonetheless, about one-third of young cheetahs still fall

victim to other predators, especially hyenas, during this period.

After three months, the cubs accompany their mother while she hunts. Because the cubs are still playful, they often frighten away intended prey. Somewhere between fifteen and seventeen months of age, the cubs separate from their mother.

Throughout history, people have made use of the cheetah's hunting skills. By about 3000 B.C., for example, the Sumerians had domesticated cheetahs and learned to use them for hunting. Later, around 1500 B.C., the Egyptian pharaohs also used cheetahs for hunting. And in the late Middle Ages, hunting with cheetahs was fashionable in Europe. Kaiser Leopold I of Austria, for instance, hunted rabbits and deer with cheetahs around 1700.

Cheetahs once lived throughout Africa and southern Asia. But their numbers have been severely reduced, and in some areas, cheetahs have completely disappeared. Since

Cheetah Subgroups

1. South African cheetah	*Acinonyx jubatus jubatus*
2. Royal cheetah	*Acinonyx jubatus rex*
3. Tanzanian cheetah	*Acinonyx jubatus ngorongorensis*
4. Kenyan cheetah	*Acinonyx jubatus velox*
5. Sudanese cheetah	*Acinonyx jubatus soemmeringi*
6. North African cheetah	*Acinonyx jubatus hecki*
7. Indian cheetah	*Acinonyx jubatus venaticus* (extinct 1947)
8. Caspian cheetah	*Acinonyx jubatus raddei*

Cheetah cubs wander warily in the tall savanna grass, watching for their mother's return.

the thin, bristly coat of the cheetah has had little demand with people, these cats have never been hunted in great numbers. They have been much more seriously endangered by hunters who have captured them for zoos and safari parks. Until the 1950s, cheetahs did not reproduce in captivity, so new animals continually had to be captured in the wild.

Today, the main threat to the cheetah is the continuing destruction of the African savanna, which is their habitat. The population of cheetahs fell from thirty thousand in 1960 to about fifteen thousand in 1972. By 1980, there were probably fewer than ten thousand. Despite intensive efforts to save them, all indications are that the cheetah population will continue to dwindle.

Eight cheetah subspecies have been identified. The subgroups are designated on the basis of geographic location. All cheetahs look very much alike. Only the royal cheetah is somewhat different. Its black spots appear as formless patches arranged in stripes down its back.

APPENDIX
TO
ANIMAL FAMILIES

BIG CATS

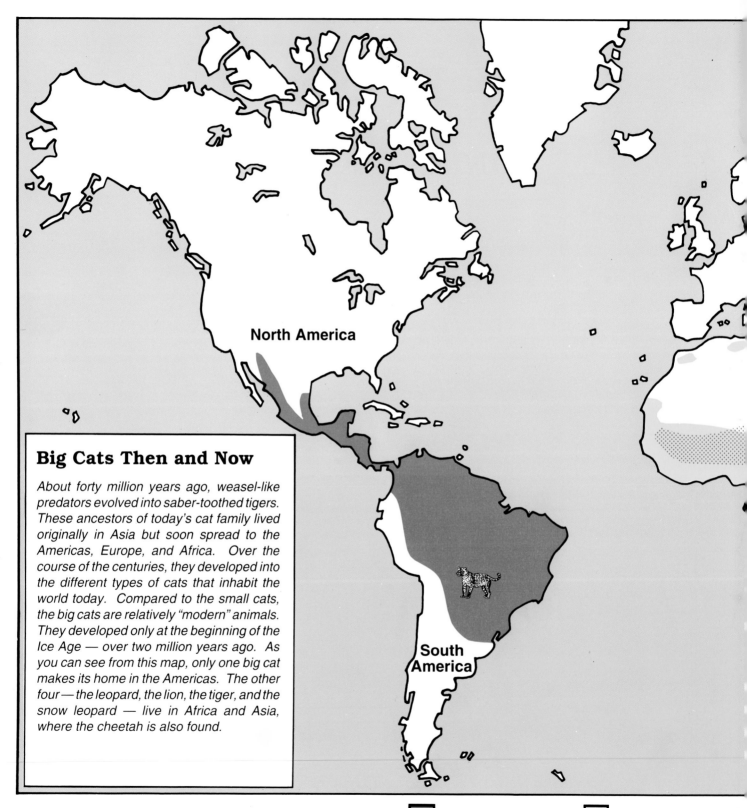

North America

Big Cats Then and Now

About forty million years ago, weasel-like predators evolved into saber-toothed tigers. These ancestors of today's cat family lived originally in Asia but soon spread to the Americas, Europe, and Africa. Over the course of the centuries, they developed into the different types of cats that inhabit the world today. Compared to the small cats, the big cats are relatively "modern" animals. They developed only at the beginning of the Ice Age — over two million years ago. As you can see from this map, only one big cat makes its home in the Americas. The other four — the leopard, the lion, the tiger, and the snow leopard — live in Africa and Asia, where the cheetah is also found.

South America

Jaguar

Leopard

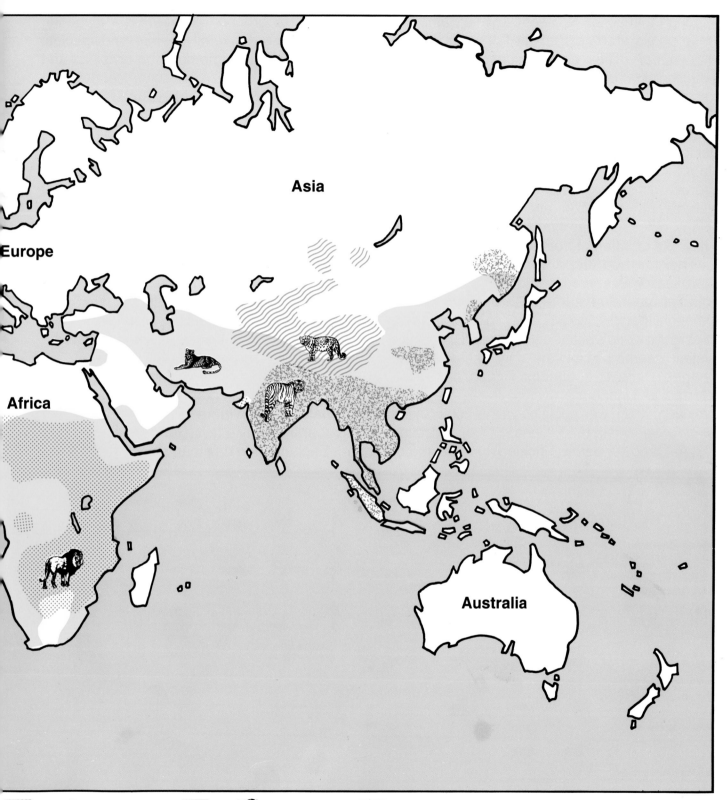

Asia

Europe

Africa

Australia

Lion

Tiger

Snow leopard

43

ABOUT THESE BOOKS

Although this series is called "Animal Families," these books aren't just about fathers, mothers, and young. They also discuss the scientific definition of *family*, which is a division of biological classification and includes many animals.

Biological classification is a method that scientists use to identify and organize living things. Using this system, scientists place animals and plants into larger groups that share similar characteristics. Characteristics are physical features, natural habits, ancestral backgrounds, or any other qualities that make one organism either like or different from another.

The method used today for biological classification was introduced in 1753 by a Swedish botanist-naturalist named Carolus Linnaeus. Although many scientists tried to find ways to classify the world's plants and animals, Linnaeus's system seemed to be the only useful choice. Charles Darwin, a famous British naturalist, referred to Linnaeus's system in his theory of evolution, which was published in his book *On the Origin of Species* in 1859. Linnaeus's classification system, shown below, includes seven major categories, or groups. These are: kingdom, phylum, class, order, family, genus, and species.

An easy way to remember the divisions and their order is to memorize this sentence: "Ken Put Cake On Frank's Good Shirt." The first letter of each word in the sentence gives you the first letter of a division. (The *K* in *Ken*, for example, stands for *kingdom*.) The order of the words in the sentence suggests the order of the divisions from largest to smallest. The kingdom is the largest of these divisions; the species is the smallest. The larger the division, the more types of animals or plants it contains. For example, the animal kingdom, called Animalia, contains everything from worms to whales. Smaller divisions, such as the family, have fewer members that share more characteristics. For example, members of the bear family, Ursidae, include the polar bear, the brown bear, and many others.

In the following chart, the lion species is followed through all seven categories. As the categories expand to include more and more members, remember that only a few examples are pictured here. Each division has many more members.

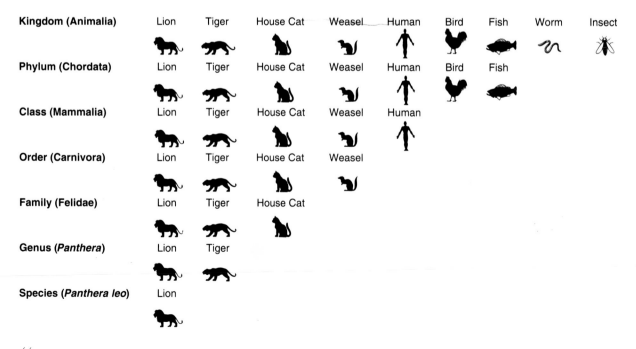

	Lion	Tiger	House Cat	Weasel	Human	Bird	Fish	Worm	Insect
Kingdom (Animalia)	Lion	Tiger	House Cat	Weasel	Human	Bird	Fish	Worm	Insect
Phylum (Chordata)	Lion	Tiger	House Cat	Weasel	Human	Bird	Fish		
Class (Mammalia)	Lion	Tiger	House Cat	Weasel	Human				
Order (Carnivora)	Lion	Tiger	House Cat	Weasel					
Family (Felidae)	Lion	Tiger	House Cat						
Genus (*Panthera*)	Lion	Tiger							
Species (*Panthera leo*)	Lion								

SCIENTIFIC NAMES OF THE ANIMALS IN THIS BOOK

Animals have different names in every language. For this reason, researchers the world over use the same scientific names, which usually stem from ancient Greek or Latin. Most animals are classified by two names. One is the genus name; the other is the name of the species to which they belong. Additional names indicate further subgroupings. Here is a list of the animals included in *Big Cats*.

Tiger	*Panthera tigris*
Lion	*Panthera leo*
Leopard	*Panthera pardus*
Jaguar	*Panthera onca*
Snow leopard	*Panthera uncia*
Cheetah	*Acinonyx jubatus*

(For further subgroups of these species, see the charts in the individual sections.)

GLOSSARY

botanist
A scientist who studies plants.

carnivore
A predominantly meat-eating animal.

carrion
The decaying flesh of a dead animal; a carcass. Jackals, vultures, hyenas, and many other animals feed on carrion as a source of food.

class
The third of seven divisions in the biological classification system proposed by the Swedish botanist-naturalist Carolus Linnaeus. The class is the main subdivision of the phylum. Cats belong to the class Mammalia, which includes humans.

environment
The conditions, circumstances, and influences affecting the development of an animal or group of animals.

evolution
The gradual process of change that occurs in any organism and its descendants over time. Organisms evolve to survive the changes that can occur in climate, food supply, air quality, and other such factors.

extinction
The end or destruction of a specific type of living organism (plant or animal).

family
The fifth of seven divisions in the biological classification system proposed by the Swedish botanist-naturalist Carolus Linnaeus. The family is the main subdivision of the order and contains one or more genera. Cats — big, small, wild, and domestic — belong to the family known as Felidae.

genus (plural: **genera**)
The sixth of seven divisions in the biological classification system proposed by Swedish botanist-naturalist Carolus Linnaeus. A genus is the main subdivision of a family and includes one or more species. At this level, big cats form their own group, known as *Panthera*.

gestation period
The number of days from the conception of to the birth of an animal. Gestation periods vary greatly for different types of animals.

habitat
The natural living area or environment in which an animal usually lives.

hemisphere
One of the two halves into which the earth is divided by the equator.

herbivore
An animal whose diet consists mainly of plants.

hyenas
A group of wolflike, flesh-eating animals that live in Africa and Asia. Hyenas are known for their scavenging habits. But recent studies show that they live primarily off of prey they capture themselves.

hyoid bone
A bone at the base of the tongue that supports the tongue and its muscles. In animals such as cats, this bone is shaped like a *T*. In humans, this bone has a shape like a *U*.

jackal
A yellowish gray meat-eating wild dog of Asia and northern Africa. Jackals are smaller than wolves. They travel in packs and hunt their prey at night.

kingdom
The first of seven divisions in the biological classification system proposed by the Swedish botanist-naturalist Carolus Linnaeus. Animals, including human beings, belong to the kingdom Animalia.

marten
A meat-eating animal related to the weasel.

naturalist
A person who studies and observes plants and animals in their natural settings.

nocturnal
Active at night and usually asleep during the day.

omnivore
An animal that eats both animals and plants.

order
The fourth of seven divisions in the biological classification system proposed by the Swedish botanist-naturalist Carolus Linnaeus. The order is the main subdivision of the class and contains many different families. Big cats, for example, belong to the order known as Carnivora. This order is shared by meat-eating animal families such as that of the bear, dog, hyena, and weasel.

phylum (plural: phyla)
The second of seven divisions in the biological classification system proposed by the Swedish botanist-naturalist Carolus Linnaeus. A phylum is one of the main divisions of a kingdom. Big cats belong to the phylum Chordata, a group consisting mostly of animals with backbones (vertebrates).

predator
An animal that lives by eating other animals.

prey
Any creature hunted or caught as food.

puma
A long-tailed, slender, yellowish brown animal of the cat family. The puma, also known as the cougar or mountain lion, is found in North and South America.

sanctuary
A reservation for animals. In sanctuaries, animals are sheltered for breeding purposes and may not be hunted or otherwise molested.

savanna
A type of tropical or subtropical prairie. Savannas are common in central Africa.

serval
A small member of the cat family found mainly in southern Africa. The serval's features include a long, ringed tail, long legs, and large ears.

species
The last of seven divisions in the biological classification system proposed by the Swedish botanist-naturalist Carolus Linnaeus. The species is the main subdivision of the genus. It may include further subgroups of its own, called subspecies. At the level of species, members share many features and are capable of breeding with one another.

taiga
The cone-bearing forests in the far northern regions of Europe, Asia, and North America. Big cats are known to live and roam in these areas.

zoologist
A scientist who studies animals.

MORE BOOKS ABOUT BIG CATS

African Lion. Carl R. Green and William R. Sanford (Crestwood House)
The Bengal Tiger. Carl R. Green and William R. Sanford (Crestwood House)
Big Cats. Wildlife Education Ltd. Staff (Wildlife Education)
Jane Goodall's Animal World: Lions. Leslie MacGuire with Jane Goodall, editor (Macmillan)
Lion Prides and Tiger Tracks. Don Torgersen (Childrens Press)
Lions and Tigers. Lionel Bender (Franklin Watts)
Where the Leopard Passes. Sheila Hawkins (Schocken)
Wonders of Tigers. Sigmund A. Lavine (Putnam)
A Year in the Life of a Tiger. John Stidworthy (Silver, Burdett & Ginn)

PLACES TO WRITE

The following are some of the many organizations that exist to educate people about animals, promote the protection of animals, and encourage the conservation of their environments. Write to these organizations for more information about big cats, other animals, or animal concerns of interest to you. When you write, include your name, address, and age, and tell them clearly what you want to know. Don't forget to enclose a stamped, self-addressed envelope for a reply.

African Wildlife Foundation
1717 Massachusetts Avenue NW
Washington, D.C. 20036

Elsa Clubs of America
P.O. Box 4572
North Hollywood, California
91617-0572

Rainforest Action Network
301 Broadway, Suite A
San Francisco, California 94133

Unexpected Wildlife Foundation
P.O. Box 765
Newfield, New Jersey 08344

World Wildlife Fund (Canada)
90 Eglinton Avenue East, Suite 504
Toronto, Ontario M4P 2Z7

World Wildlife Fund (U.S.)
1250 24th Street NW
Washington, D.C. 20037

THINGS TO DO

These projects are designed to help you have fun with what you've learned about big cats. You can do them alone, in small groups, or as a class project.

1. Now that you have read *Big Cats*, spend a day at the zoo. How many big cats can you identify?

2. Using an encyclopedia or other reference, compare and contrast photographs and vital statistics of big and small cats. If you can find pictures or diagrams of their bone structures, compare them, too.

3. Have you ever considered becoming a naturalist, a biologist, a veterinarian, or other animal-related scientist? Investigate these professions and see what training is necessary to work in these fields.

4. Find your home (country, state, province) on the map in this book. Do any big cats make their homes in your area? If not, what type of big cat is found nearest you? Find out what (if any) big cats roamed the area in which you live in the past. When did they disappear from that area? Why?

INDEX

201008

TOWNSHIP OF LIBRARY
BIBLIOTHEQUE PUBLIQUE DU CANTON DE RUSSELL
SUCC. RUSSELL BRANCH

BIBLIOTHEQUE PUBLIQUE DU CANTON DE RUSSELL
TOWNSHIP OF RUSSELL PUBLIC LIBRARY
SUCC. MARIONVILLE BRANCH